T0159076

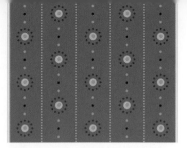

Classic Recipes of
BRAZIL

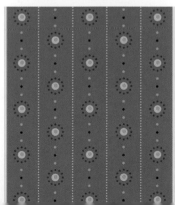

Classic Recipes of
BRAZIL

TRADITIONAL FOOD AND COOKING
IN 25 AUTHENTIC DISHES

FERNANDO FARAH

LORENZ BOOKS

This edition is published by
Lorenz Books,
an imprint of Anness Publishing Ltd,
108 Great Russell Street,
London WC1B 3NA

www.lorenzbooks.com;
www.annesspublishing.com

If you like the images in this book and
would like to investigate using them for
publishing, promotions or advertising,
please visit our website
www.practicalpictures.com for more
information.

Publisher: Joanna Lorenz
Editor: Joanne Rippin & Helen Sudell
Designer: Nigel Partridge
Production Controller: Mai-Ling Collyer
Recipe Photography: William Lingwood

The image on the front cover is of Leão
Veloso Fish Soup, page 30.

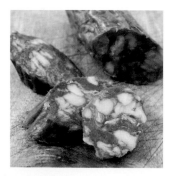

A CIP catalogue record for this book is
available from the British Library

PUBLISHER'S NOTE

Although the advice and information in this
book are believed to be accurate and true
at the time of going to press, neither the
authors nor the publisher can accept any
legal responsibility or liability for any errors
or omissions that may have been made nor
for any inaccuracies nor for any loss, harm
or injury that comes about from following
instructions or advice in this book.

PUBLISHER'S ACKNOWLEDGMENTS

The Publisher would like to thank the
following agencies for the use of their
images. Alamy: p10 top right, p11 top right.
Fotalia: p6, p7 bottom left, p8.

COOK'S NOTES

Bracketed terms are intended for American
readers. For all recipes, quantities are given
in both metric and imperial measures and,
where appropriate, in standard cups and
spoons. Follow one set of measures, but
not a mixture, because they are not
interchangeable.

Standard spoon and cup measures are
level. 1 tsp = 5ml, 1 tbsp = 15ml, 1 cup =
250ml/8fl oz. Australian standard
tablespoons are 20ml. Australian readers
should use 3 tsp in place of 1 tbsp for
measuring small quantities.

American pints are 16fl oz/2 cups.
American readers should use 20fl oz/2.5
cups in place of 1 pint when measuring
liquids.

Electric oven temperatures in this book are
for conventional ovens. When using a fan
oven, the temperature will probably need to
be reduced by about 10–20°C/20–40°F.
Since ovens vary, you should check with
your manufacturer's instruction book for
guidance.

The nutritional analysis given for each
recipe is calculated per portion (i.e. serving
or item), unless otherwise stated. If the
recipe gives a range, such as Serves 4–6,
then the nutritional analysis will be for the
smaller portion size, i.e. 6 servings. The
analysis does not include optional
ingredients, such as salt added to taste.

Medium (US large) eggs are used unless
otherwise stated.

Contents

Introduction

Brazil is a country of dazzling beauty, with a wide variety of different climates and ecosystems. With a richly fertile land, a lush coastline, and some of the longest rivers in the world, Brazil has the means to supply itself with almost every kind of ingredient. The country is also home to a population of great ethnic and cultural diversity. Brazilian cuisine combines the dishes of its native inhabitants with flavours from Portugal, Africa, the Middle East and East Asia, as immigrants have arrived from these countries over the centuries, bringing their unique food traditions with them.

Left: The fabulous sight of Rio de Janeiro's famous beaches, where vendors serve delicious snacks and cooling drinks.

Brazilian Cuisine

For many Brazilians, their passion for life is expressed through family, food, the beach, carnival and football. Football fans will meet at bars before the game and fill up on snacks such as *pastel*, a deep-fried filled pastry. All along the coast, beach kiosks and street vendors battle to outdo each other, providing fresh coconut water, iced tea, cassava cookies, fruit, grilled cheese or coconut tapioca pudding.

Below: Pastels are popular street food all over Brazil and can be filled with meat or vegetables.

Above: A traditional farofas accompanies many meat or fish dishes.

Brazilian eating traditions

Whether at home or in a restaurant, meals are seen as not just a time to eat, but also for spending time with family and friends. Breakfast may be a simple meal of bread and butter with coffee and fresh fruit, but lunch is usually a sit-down meal, which can last more than an hour. The evening meal, therefore is served late.

One of the favourite eating experiences in Brazil is the *churrascaria*. These are large restaurants specializing in *churrasco* – grilled meats – that can feed two to three hundred people per session. A home-made churrasco usually involves multiple chunks of premium cuts such as best beef steak, ribs, pork loin, coarse pork sausages, chicken breast or even cured cheese, impaled on large skewers and seasoned with nothing more than rock salt, then cooked over a charcoal grill. Guests bring myriad side dishes to accompany the meat, such as *farofas* (cassava flour toasted in butter) rice, beans, deep-fried bananas, corn and many others.

Another favourite meal is the *feijoada* – pork and bean stew – where the meat is soaked overnight, then simmered in large pans for several hours with dried black beans. An hour or so before serving, the feijoada is seasoned with fried onions and garlic. Side dishes of rice, (bell) peppers and oranges accompany the meat.

Right: A good churrasco is an excuse to eat fabulously grilled meats of all kinds.

Feasts and Festivals

Brazil has a rich folklore. Throughout its massive territory, Brazil's myriad communities celebrate their inherited culture in different ways. There are hundreds of colourful festivals, carnivals, processions, pilgrimages and even group blessings, most of which involve delicious food and drink.

Semena Santa

Holy week is a Catholic celebration that starts on the Sunday before Easter Sunday. Tradition dictates that red meat should be avoided on Good Friday. Many families cook a

Below: Salt cod is traditionally eaten on Good Friday.

large fish or opt for *bacalhau* (salt cod), originally a Portuguese favourite.

Festa Junina

The tradition of *Festa Junina* (June Festivals) celebrates three of the most well-loved Catholic saints in Brazil: St John, St Peter and St Antony. In the north-east it is also a celebration of the arrival of winter and the start of the much-needed rainy season. The corn harvest is under way, so corn features in most of the traditional treats found at June parties: *pamonha* (corn pudding steamed in corn husks), maize couscous, *curau* (corn custard), cooked or grilled corn, maize cakes and popcorn.

European, African and Oriental traditions have also been adopted. Square dancing comes from Portugal and Spain, fireworks and flying lanterns were originally Chinese, and from Africa, there are sweet treats such as *mugunzá* (hominy corn porridge), *cocada* (coconut and sugar bar) and *pé de moleque* (peanut brittle).

Above: Festival flags at São Luís Historic City celebrate St John.

Christmas

As it comes right in the middle of Brazil's summer it makes sense to celebrate Christmas in the evening. The main meal is therefore held on the night of Christmas Eve.

Despite the high temperatures, roast turkey is the most popular festive meal, prepared with a stuffing of farofa mixed with dried fruit and chestnuts, and accompanied by white rice and gravy. Sweet glazed ham is another favourite and can be served hot or cold. One peculiar tradition is the habit of decorating the turkey with *fios d'ovos* (egg strings), a Portuguese delicacy made by dribbling egg yolk on boiling sugar syrup.

For desserts, many Brazilians will tuck into *rabanada*, a distant cousin of French toast, made with thick slices of bread covered with a generous layer of sugar and cinnamon.

New Year's Eve

Brazilians use the French word 'Reveillon' instead of New Year's Eve, and it is celebrated with great enthusiasm. Reveillon dinner is usually a very luxurious meal, with preference given to dishes that can be served cold during this hot season, such as cold meats, terrines, savoury mousses, pies, salads and plenty of fruit. There are numerous superstitions associated with the day, such as not eating poultry (as they walk backwards while pecking for food), or chewing seven pomegranate seeds and keeping their husks in a piece of paper concealed in your wallet to attract good fortune in the coming year.

Above: Carnival is a time to dress up and party!

Carnival

In late February or early March, the whole country's attention turns to carnival – a four-day long celebration of music, dance, eating and drinking. Rio's carnivals may be world-famous, but there are street parties in every town. Food is kept to light dishes with plenty of cold cuts and fresh fruit, and revellers are kept cool by consuming large amounts of freezing cold beer, *batidas* and *caipirinhas*.

Caipirinha

Brazil's most famous cocktail. Serve on ice.

Makes 1

½ lime, cut into wedges
30ml/2 tbsp caster (superfine) sugar
250ml/8fl oz/1 cup crushed ice
50ml/2fl oz/¼ cup cachaça

Place the wedges in the glass, with the sugar. Use a cocktail muddler to crush the lime and sugar together, to release the oils from the lime skin and dissolve the sugar in the lime juice. Top the glass with the crushed ice, then pour in the cachaça. Stir and serve.

Classic Ingredients

Brazil is a rich and productive country, and the sheer variety of fruits, vegetables, fish and meat here is amazing.

Meat, poultry and game

Two kinds of meat reign supreme in Brazil: beef and pork. The best beef is served quite simply as a juicy steak, while lesser cuts are stewed gently with vegetables or turned into *carne seca* (Brazilian beef jerky or dried beef). There are two types of pork sausage in Brazil: *salsicha* (processed meat sausages resembling frankfurters) and *linguiça* (a

Below: Salted dried shrimp adds depth and flavour to stews.

sausage with visible large meat chunks). Salsichas are usually used for hot dogs, and linguiças are delicious when fried, cut and served like cocktail sausages. Thicker versions (often called *calabresa*) feature in summer barbecues or one of the meats in a feijoada.

Fish and shellfish

Many of the sea and river fish eaten in Brazil are known only in that country. Luckily, the kinds of white fish available everywhere can be substituted for the local Brazilian fish with a similar result. For example, try a mixture of cod, haddock, plaice or turbot in a mixed fish stew or fish soup. The sauces surrounding the fish are all-important, the individual flavour of each fish less so. Brazil produces a huge quantity of prawns (shrimp) in its seaside farms and they feature in many stews and soups.

Vegetables

Nearly all Brazilians eat fresh or dried beans on a daily basis. Black beans appear as a main

ingredient of Brazil's national dish, feijoada. Corn is the most popular grain in Brazil. As a fresh product it is used in recipes such as curau (corn custard). It is also milled into flour (*fubá*), which is used in *bolo de Fubá* (maize cake) and polenta (corn meal mash), which is served with stews.

Cassava, or manioc, is a root vegetable that grows abundantly in Brazil. Cassava is poisonous raw but the root itself and both types of flour it produces are consumed in huge amounts. The root is boiled as a replacement for potatoes, or deep fried as chips (fries). Cassava flour is used to thicken sauces, or add crunch to stews or beans. It is also served simply toasted with butter, and mixed with other ingredients to make farofa. The pure starch, *polvinho*, is available in sweet and sour varieties and is used to make tapioca pancakes.

Right: Cornmeal is very popular in Brazil and is used primarily to make polenta.

Above: Açaí pulp features in desserts and healthy drinks.

Fruit and nuts

The exotic fruits found growing in Brazil are now well known in other parts of the world. Guavas are native fruits of Central and South America and are readily available as white and red-fleshed varieties. The white guava is most commonly eaten raw, while the red variety is made into *goiabada*, a thick guava preserve available in many textures, from soft and spreadable to a solid block sometimes called guava cheese. Açaí is the berry of the açaí palm, native to the tropical north of Brazil. The deep blue-purple pulp is separated from the pip,

then mashed and frozen for storage. Açaí berries are high in antioxidants and açaí juice is a popular health drink.

Avocados are very plentiful in Brazil. They are larger than the Hess variety, with a very light, sweet flesh, which explains why most Brazilians see it as a dessert fruit.

The humble lime is a must-have in every Brazilian house. it is used as a marinade for fish or pork, as well as for making juices, cocktails, sorbets, desserts and cakes. Finally, the most-used ingredient after cassava must be the coconut; its flesh featuring in many sweet and savoury Brazilian dishes, and its water used for a refreshing health drink.

Peanuts are planted in vast quantities throughout Brazil and peanut oil is popular in cooking. The nuts are used in peanut brittle or sold freshly roasted by street vendors. The *caju* (cashew) nut is a popular appetizer and Brazil nuts, called *castanhas do pará*, are the largest export from the Amazon.

Above: Coconut and its milk flavour many Brazilian desserts.

Dairy

There are many kinds of cheese in Brazil, usually pale in colour and sold while still fresh rather than matured. For example, *queijo minas* is a fresh curd cheese, sold within days of manufacture in sealed pots that retain the whey. It is used in sandwiches, salads and desserts. *Queijo coalho* is a firm, lightweight cheese, quite salty in taste and similar to Greek halloumi. It is often found on street stalls, freshly grilled.

Catipury is the brand name of Brazil's most famous *requeijão*, a processed cheese halfway between cheese and cream.

It appears everywhere, from the filling for the country's favourite snack, pastel, to the sauce for guava soufflé. Catupiry is rarely available outside Brazil, but a soft curd or cream cheese is an acceptable substitute.

Liete moça (condensed milk) is incredibly popular in Brazil. It is used in hundreds of recipes, from a traditional *Pudim de Leite* (caramel custard) to fresh fruit cocktails.

Hot pepper sauce

Known in Portugal and Mozambique as piri piri, the *malugueta* pepper is a small green (bell) pepper that turns

Below: Highly spiced red pepper sauce is used at barbecues.

Above: These wonderful truffles are made with Liete Moça.

red as it ripens, and packs quite a punch. The sauce is often brought to the table in small pots, infused in oil, to be added to the plate by each diner.

Drinks

Both alcoholic concoctions and non-alcoholic soft drinks are consumed in quantities in this hot country. The juice bars in major cities and towns are marvellous sources of all kinds of fruit drinks based on the produce of the countryside. When it comes to something more alcoholic, the most popular spirit sold in Brazil is cachaça, a liquor distilled from

sugar cane. It is the main ingredient of Brazil's favourite cocktail, caipirinha, made with cachaça, sugar and lime.

In the south, the favourite hot drink is *mate*, consumed from calabash gourds and sipped through a metal spoon with strainer holes at the bottom. Iced mate is a hugely popular drink, served by vendors who carry drums of it up and down the beaches.

Brazil is the world's biggest producer and exporter of coffee, with an enormous harvest from its colonial plantations. It is drunk several times a day in tiny cups with plenty of sugar.

Below: Coffee is normally taken black and very sweet.

A Passion for Food

Brazilian food, like its peoples and culture, is colourful, eclectic and tastes fabulous. From irresistible snacks like *Pastel de Feira* (little filled pastries) or *Aipim Frito* (cassava chips), to hearty main meals such as *Arroz de Carreteiro* (beef jerky risotto), these authentic regional dishes are eaten and loved by cooks in city restaurants, rural farmhouses and private homes throughout Brazil. Choose a main course, pair it with cheese and bread, and you have a simple supper, or go all-out and make a traditional feijoada – the black bean and pork feast – and invite the entire family round for a splendid Brazilian celebration of life.

Left: Many Brazilians have a sweet tooth and love all kinds of cakes and desserts.

Green Broth Caldo verde

1 Heat the oil in a large pan over a medium heat. Add the onion and cook gently for 8–10 minutes, until soft. Add the garlic and half the chouriço and cook for 2 minutes, stirring.

2 Add the potatoes and water, bring to the boil, then lower the heat, half-cover the pan with a lid and simmer for 15 minutes, or until the potatoes are just tender. Remove from the heat and set aside to cool for 5 minutes.

3 Purée the soup in a food processor or blender, in batches, if necessary, then pour back into the pan. Add the spring greens, bring to the boil, cover and simmer for 2–3 minutes, or until tender.

4 Season to taste with salt and pepper and ladle into warmed bowls. Serve piping hot, garnished with the remaining cubes of chouriço and a drizzle of olive oil.

COOK'S TIP
When preparing the spring greens, remove the tough stalks, then roll each leaf up tightly and shred as finely as possible with a sharp knife.

Serves 6
60ml/4 tbsp olive oil, plus extra to
    drizzle
1 large onion, chopped
2 cloves garlic, finely chopped
200g/7oz chouriço, or chorizo, cubed
675g/1½ lb potatoes, peeled and
    diced
2 litres/3½ pints/8 cups cold water
350g/12oz spring greens (collards),
    finely shredded
salt and ground black pepper

Originally from Portugal, caldo verde is a light soup that is well suited to the mild winters of Brazil's southern states. The broth, combined with the peppery taste of the spring greens and smoky chouriço sausage, makes this sophisticated comfort food. If you can't find Portuguese chouriço, use Spanish chorizo instead.

Black Bean Pick-me-up Caldinho de feijão

Serves 6

15ml/1 tbsp vegetable oil

225g/8oz bacon lardons, or crumbled pork scratchings

450g/1lb Everyday Black Beans (see page 45)

250ml/8fl oz/1 cup water

salt and ground black pepper

olive oil, to drizzle

30ml/2 tbsp fresh parsley, chopped

1 Heat the vegetable oil in a deep frying pan and fry the bacon lardons until crispy. Transfer to a plate lined with kitchen paper to drain, and allow to cool.

2 Put the black beans and water in a food processor or blender and season with salt and pepper. Blend to a smooth purée.

3 Pour into a small pan, bring to the boil and simmer for 5 minutes.

4 Pour or ladle the soup into small heatproof glasses or porcelain espresso cups. Garnish with a drizzle of olive oil, a generous sprinkling of chopped parsley and bacon lardons or crumbled pork scratchings. Serve piping hot.

Although it sounds unusual, little shots of soup are often served at Brazilian bars to accompany your drink, and they go surprisingly well with cold beer and cocktails. This tasty version is made more substantial with the addition of crispy bacon.

Deep-fried Chunky Cassava chips Aipim frito

Serves 6

1 large cassava root, about 675g/
   1½ lb in weight
1 onion
24 whole cloves
30ml/2 tbsp salt, plus extra for
   serving
vegetable oil for deep-frying

Cassava grows well in hot and humid climates, and features in many Brazilian recipes from main courses to desserts, bread and cakes. Because it has a high starch content, it makes delicious chips that are crunchy on the outside and fluffy in the middle, so an evening out often begins with an order of this popular bar snack.

1 Peel the cassava and cut across its width into three chunks. Peel the onion and spike it with the cloves, then put it in a large pan. Add plenty of water to the pan – you'll need about 3 litres/5¼ pints/12 cups – and add the salt. Add the cassava root and bring to the boil.

2 Turn down the heat, half cover the pan and simmer for 20 minutes, or until the cassava is tender. Drain and set aside to cool. When cool, insert a small knife into the chunks and twist them open. Remove any tough fibres from the middle of the cassava chunks and discard. Cut the cassava into chip-sized wedges.

3 Heat a 7.5cm/3in depth of vegetable oil in a deep pan until it registers 190°C/375°F on a sugar thermometer. Fry in batches for 3 minutes. Drain and set aside to cool. After all the wedges are fried and cooled, reheat the oil and fry again until golden and crispy. Drain and place on a plate lined with kitchen paper. Add salt and serve immediately.

Salt Cod Fritters Bolinho de bacalhau

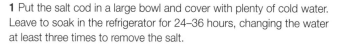

Makes about 25
450g/1lb salt cod
400g/14oz/2 cups cold mashed
  potatoes
15ml/1 tbsp finely chopped fresh
  parsley
3 eggs, separated
15ml/1 tbsp olive oil
115g/4oz/1 cup dry breadcrumbs
ground black pepper
vegetable oil for deep-frying
lime wedges and hot pepper sauce,
  to serve

1 Put the salt cod in a large bowl and cover with plenty of cold water. Leave to soak in the refrigerator for 24–36 hours, changing the water at least three times to remove the salt.

2 Drain the cod and place in a pan with fresh cold water. Bring to the boil, lower the heat and simmer for 15 minutes. Drain and set the fish aside to cool. When the fish is cold, discard any skin and bones, place in a food processor and pulse a few times to shred; do not purée.

3 Put the shredded fish, mashed potatoes, chopped parsley, egg yolks and olive oil in a bowl. Season with pepper and mix well.

4 In a separate bowl, whisk the egg whites until stiff peaks form, then carefully fold them into the fish and potato mixture.

5 Put the breadcrumbs in a wide shallow bowl or on a plate.

6 Using a tablespoon, scoop up the mixture into walnut-sized balls and roll between the palms of your hands. Roll a few balls at a time in the breadcrumbs to coat, then transfer to a baking tray. Chill in the refrigerator for 30 minutes to firm them up.

7 Heat a 7.5cm/3in depth of vegetable oil in a deep, heavy pan to 180°C/350°F on a sugar thermometer. Fry the salt cod fritters in small batches until golden. Drain on kitchen paper, transfer to a baking tray, and keep warm in a low oven while cooking the rest.

8 Serve with hot pepper sauce and garnished with lime wedges.

Brazilians love their salgadinhos (appetizers), which are eaten as snacks throughout the day. Portuguese in origin, these delicious salt cod fritters can be found wherever ice-cold beer is served. You will need to begin this dish a day or two in advance to allow time to soak the fish.

Deep-fried Pastry with Cheese Filling
Pastel de feira de queijo

1 To make the pastry, sift the flour and salt into a large bowl. Rub in the lard with your fingertips until the mixture resembles fine breadcrumbs. Stir in the cachaça and white vinegar, then gradually mix in the warm water a little at a time until the mixture forms a rough, dry dough.

2 Transfer to a lightly floured surface and knead for 3–4 minutes until you have a smooth but fairly stiff dough. Shape into a roll with a diameter of about 5cm/1 in. Wrap in clear film (plastic wrap) and leave at room temperature for at least 4 hours.

3 Cut the dough into six pieces. Using a rolling pin or pasta machine, roll each piece until a little thinner than 3mm/⅛ in, then trim into a 10 x 20cm/4 x 8 in rectangle. Use straight away, or make a stack of rectangles, adding baking parchment between each layer.

4 Tightly cover the whole stack with clear film and refrigerate until needed. You can store the dough for up to four days before using.

5 Place the six pastry rectangles on a floured surface and lightly brush the edges with water.

6 Put a heaped tablespoonful of grated cheese in the centre of one half of each rectangle, and fold the other half over it. Firmly press the edges together, then, using a fork, mark a pattern all around the edges.

7 Heat a 7.5cm/3in depth of vegetable oil in a deep pan to 190°C/375°F on a sugar thermometer. Fry the pastries, one at a time until golden and crisp. Use metal slotted spoons to turn them over every 30 seconds, so that they brown on both sides.

8 Drain on kitchen paper and keep warm in a low oven while cooking the remainder. Serve hot with salsa, Worcestershire sauce, hot pepper sauce, ketchup or chutney.

Makes 6
200g/9½ oz/scant 2¾ cups plain (all-purpose) flour
5ml/1 tsp salt
30ml/2 tbsp lard or white cooking fat, diced
5ml/1 tsp cachaça or vodka
15ml/1 tbsp white vinegar
120ml/4fl oz/½ cup warm water
Brazilian-style Salsa (see page 50), Worcestershire sauce, hot pepper sauce, ketchup or chutney, to serve

For the filling
200g/7oz/2 cups grated (shredded) mozzarella

Mozzarella cheese is classic pastel (little pastry) filling. You could also try a pizza-like version with cheese, chopped tomatoes and fresh oregano.

Stuffed Baked Crabs Casquinha de siri

Serves 8

2 slices day-old white bread
75ml/5 tbsp milk
15ml/1 tbsp olive oil
1 shallot, finely chopped
1 clove garlic, crushed
1 large tomato, peeled, seeded and
  chopped
90ml/6 tbsp white wine
45ml/3 tbsp butter, plus extra for
  greasing
450g/1lb white crab meat
15g/½oz/¼ cup chopped fresh
  coriander (cilantro)
5ml/1 tsp chopped parsley
1.5ml/¼ tsp grated nutmeg
2.5ml/½ tsp palm oil (dendê)
15ml/1 tbsp double (heavy) cream
65g/2½oz/generous ½ cup fine dry
  breadcrumbs
40g/1½oz/⅜ cup Parmesan cheese,
  grated
wedges of lime and hot pepper
  sauce, to serve

COOK'S TIP

Palm oil, known in Brazil as dendé oil, is a thick, reddish, strong-flavoured oil extracted from the pulp of a fruit from a palm tree grown in Brazil. Substitute the palm oil with annato or peanut oil, if you prefer.

1 Put the bread on a shallow plate or in a small bowl and spoon over the milk. Leave to soak for a few minutes. Lightly grease eight clean, empty crab shells, scallop shells or shallow ramekins with butter.

2 Heat the olive oil in a pan over a medium heat. Add the shallot and fry for 2 minutes until soft. Add the garlic and fry for another minute.

3 Add the tomato and white wine to the pan, and bring to the boil. Reduce the heat and gently simmer for 5 minutes. Remove from the heat and set aside to cool.

4 Take the bread out of the milk, and squeeze it dry, then crumble it with your fingers and stir it into the tomato sauce.

5 Melt the butter over a medium heat and fry the crab meat for a few seconds. Add the tomato sauce, fresh coriander, parsley, nutmeg and palm oil. Simmer for 2 minutes, or until the mixture has little visible liquid, but is still moist. Turn off the heat, then stir in the cream.

6 Preheat the oven to 200°C/400°F/Gas 6. In a small bowl, mix together the breadcrumbs and grated Parmesan.

7 Spoon the crab mixture into the shells or ramekins and smooth the tops with the back of a spoon. Sprinkle over the Parmesan and breadcrumb mixture, and bake for 10 minutes until the tops are golden.

8 Serve straight away, accompanied by hot pepper sauce and lime wedges to squeeze over.

Crabs are plentiful in Brazil and can be found along its vast shoreline, long rivers and extensive marshlands. The 'siri' in the name of this dish refers to a large land crab mainly found in northern Brazil, and 'casquinha' refers to the crab shell that is traditionally used for serving.

Seafood and Nut Purée Vatapá

1 Tear the bread in small pieces and place in a bowl. Pour over the milk and set aside to soak.

2 Meanwhile, heat the stock in a medium pan, add the fish and poach for 3–5 minutes, depending on the thickness of the fillets, until just cooked. Remove the fish with a slotted spoon and place on a board or plate. Reserve the stock. When the fish fillets are cool enough to handle, flake and set aside.

3 Put the dried shrimp, peanuts and cashews in a food processor and blend until fine. Squeeze the bread dry and add to the processor with the fish. Blend again to a smooth purée.

4 Spoon and scrape the purée into a pan and gradually add enough of the stock to achieve a creamy consistency (you won't need it all). Add the ginger and nutmeg and season with salt and pepper to taste.

5 Cook for 3–4 minutes over a medium heat, then reduce to a simmer, stirring constantly, for 10 minutes until it becomes very thick.

6 Stir in the lime juice and palm oil, and cook for another 2 minutes, then add the coconut milk and hot pepper sauce, and cook for a further 3 or 4 minutes. Spoon into a bowl and garnish with cooked prawns and lime wedges.

This is a classic dish from the Bahia region of Brazil. It can be eaten as a main course or more usually as an accompaniment; a thicker version is good as a filling for Acarajé (black-eyed bean fritters). Vatapá may have originated in Portugal, but the use of ground nuts, coconut milk and palm oil place it firmly on the Brazilian menu.

Serves 8

½ loaf day-old French bread
500ml/17fl oz/2¼ cups milk
750ml/1¼ pints/3 cups fish stock
450g/1lb white fish fillets
65g/2½ oz dried shrimp
75g/3oz/¾ cup roasted unsalted
    peanuts
75g/3oz/¾ cup roasted cashews
2.5ml/½ tsp fresh root ginger, grated
1.5ml/¼ tsp ground nutmeg
30ml/2 tbsp lime juice
15ml/1 tbsp palm oil (dendê)
200ml/7fl oz/scant 1 cup coconut
    milk
5ml/1 tsp hot pepper sauce
salt and ground black pepper
large cooked prawns (shrimp), and
    lime wedges to garnish

Leão Veloso Fish Soup Sopa Leão Veloso

Serves 6–8

1 kg/2¼lb fresh mussels

300g/11oz raw tiger prawns (jumbo shrimp), unpeeled

1kg/2¼lb whole white fish, such as grouper, sea bass or snapper

25g/1oz/½ cup fresh parsley sprigs, plus 30ml/2 tbsp finely chopped

25g/1oz/½ cup fresh coriander (cilantro) sprigs

1 bay leaf

400g/14oz tomatoes, peeled, seeded and chopped

6 spring onions (scallions), chopped

5ml/1 tsp coriander seeds

2 cloves garlic

30ml/2 tbsp olive oil

300g/11oz white crab meat

300g/11oz cooked lobster meat

salt and ground black pepper

crusty bread, to serve

This delicious soup is named after Leão Veloso, a Brazilian ambassador who is credited with adapting the French dish, bouillabaisse, into this locally sourced Brazilian version.

1 Rinse the mussels under cold running water to help rid them of any grit, then scrub the shells to remove any barnacles. Pull off any hairy 'beards' which protrude from the side of the shell. Tap any open mussels sharply with the back of a knife. If they don't close, throw them away.

2 Shell and devein the prawns, keeping the heads and shells. Clean and fillet the fish (or ask the fishmonger to do this for you), keeping the heads and the trimmings, then cut the fillets into chunks.

3 Put the prawn shells, fish heads and trimmings in a large pan, then pour over 2.25 litres/4 pints/10 cups cold water. Add the sprigs of parsley and fresh coriander and the bay leaf. Slowly bring to boiling point, then gently simmer uncovered for 1 hour, skimming the surface occasionally, to make a stock.

4 Pour the stock through a fine sieve (strainer) or a muslin-lined colander into a bowl. Discard the prawn and fish trimmings and herbs.

5 Rinse out the pan, return the stock to it and simmer. Add the tomatoes, chopped parsley and spring onions and cook for 5 minutes.

6 Crush the coriander seeds in a spice grinder or with a mortar and pestle. Add the garlic and 5ml/1 tsp salt and grind or crush into a paste, then add to the stock.

7 Heat the oil in a deep frying pan and fry the fish and prawns until golden. Add a ladleful of the stock to the frying pan, and stir to deglaze and lift all the juices, then transfer the fish and liquid to the stock.

8 Add the crab meat, lobster meat and mussels to the stock and cook for about 5 minutes or until the mussels open. Remove any mussels that remain closed.

9 Taste and season the soup with a little more salt, if necessary, and plenty of ground black pepper. Ladle into warmed bowls and serve straight away with some bread.

Salt Cod and Potatoes Bacalhau à Gomes de Sá

1 Place the cod in a large bowl with plenty of water, and soak for 24–36 hours, changing the water at least three times.

2 Drain the cod, put in a large pan and add enough boiling water to come about 5cm/2in above the fish. Gently simmer for 20 minutes, then carefully remove the pieces of cod and set aside to cool. Keep the stock in the pan.

3 When cool enough to handle, remove any bones and skin, then flake the fish into bitesize chunks and put in a bowl.

4 Heat the milk and bay leaf until nearly boiling and pour over the fish. Leave to infuse for at least 2 hours.

5 Add the potatoes to the fish stock and bring back to the boil. Half-cover with a pan lid and simmer for 20 minutes, until tender. Drain, and when cool enough to handle, peel and cut the potatoes into 1cm/½in thick slices.

6 Transfer the cod into a colander and leave for a few minutes until well drained. Preheat the oven to 200°C/400°F/Gas 6.

7 Heat the oil in a large shallow pan and add the onions and the garlic. Gently cook for 2–3 minutes, then add the potato slices, the cod flakes and the black olives. Mix together, taking care to not flake the cod further or break too many of the potato slices. Season with freshly ground white pepper, cover and simmer for 3–4 minutes.

8 Transfer the fish mixture, sautéed onions and potatoes to a deep ceramic dish, making sure the potatoes are flat. Drizzle any olive oil left in the pan over the top. Bake for 10 minutes.

9 Remove from the oven and garnish with the chopped parsley and slices of hard-boiled egg. Serve the salt cod and potatoes with a simple green salad and crusty bread.

Serves 6

500g/1¼lb bacalhau (salt cod)
1 litre/1¾ pints/4 cups milk
1 bay leaf
500g/1¼lb medium-sized potatoes
150ml/¼ pint/⅔ cup olive oil
2 onions, sliced into rings
2 cloves garlic, sliced
175g/6oz/1 cup black olives
freshly ground white pepper
45ml/3 tbsp fresh parsley, chopped, and 2 hard-boiled eggs, sliced, to garnish
green salad and crusty bread, to serve

The Portuguese refer to salt cod as their 'faithful friend', and famously have a different recipe for every day of the year. It was an obvious choice as a non-perishable food for the three month-long voyage across the Atlantic to Brazil, and was adopted by Brazilians all over the country.

Chicken and Prawn Stew Xinxim de galinha

Serves 6

2 limes
4 cloves garlic, crushed
60ml/4 tbsp vegetable oil
1.6kg/3½lb chicken, jointed
350g/12oz raw tiger prawns (jumbo shrimp)
1 large onion, finely chopped
1 large green (bell) pepper, seeded and chopped
4 plum tomatoes, peeled, seeded and chopped
450ml/¾ pint/scant 2 cups chicken stock
40g/1½oz dried shrimp
40g/1½oz piece fresh root ginger, peeled and grated
25g/1oz/¼ cup cashew nuts
25g/1oz/¼ cup roasted unsalted peanuts
30ml/2 tbsp palm oil (dendê)
400ml/14fl oz/1¾ cups coconut milk
25g/1oz/½ cup of chopped fresh coriander (cilantro)
salt and ground black pepper
white rice and Golden Farofa (page 48), to serve

1 Whisk together the juice of 1 lime, a third of the garlic, 15ml/1 tbsp of the oil, salt and pepper in a large bowl. Add the chicken pieces and turn until coated in the mixture. Leave to marinate for at least 20 minutes.

2 Peel and devein the tiger prawns, then marinate in the juice of 1 lime, a third of the garlic, salt and pepper, for about 15 minutes.

3 Heat 15ml/1 tbsp of the oil in a large frying pan over a high heat. Add the prawns and stir-fry for 2 minutes, until just pink, but not quite cooked through. Remove and set aside.

4 Add 15ml/1 tbsp more oil to the frying pan and fry the chicken, turning frequently until golden on all sides. Remove and set aside.

5 Add the remaining 15ml/1 tbsp oil to the pan and fry the onion until soft. Add the green pepper and the rest of the garlic and fry for 1 minute. Then add the tomatoes, chicken pieces and stock and bring to the boil. Lower the heat, cover the pan and gently simmer for 30 minutes.

6 Meanwhile, in a small food processor, or with a mortar and pestle, finely grind the dried shrimp, ginger, cashew nuts and peanuts. Add to the pan and simmer for a further 5 minutes.

7 Stir in the cooked prawns, palm oil and coconut milk, then simmer for a final 3–4 minutes, or until the chicken is tender. Adjust the seasoning, if necessary. Sprinkle with fresh coriander and serve hot, accompanied by white rice and Golden Farofa.

Cooking chicken on the bone adds to the final flavour of this delicious dish. Tangy lime and spicy ginger are mellowed by creamy coconut, then fresh green peppers and tomatoes are added to the sauce – all typical ingredients of classic Brazilian cuisine.

Beef Jerky Risotto Arroz de carreteiro

1 Cut the beef jerky into 1cm/½in cubes. Place in a pan and cover with water. Bring to the boil, lower the heat and simmer for 45 minutes to 1 hour, replacing the water three times to remove excess salt.

2 In a large pan or casserole dish, heat the oil and fry the bacon lardons for one minute, then add the onion and fry for 2 minutes more until starting to soften. Add the garlic and fry for 1 more minute, stirring all the time.

3 Cut the smoked pork sausage into 1cm/½in cubes and add to the pan, together with the pre-cooked beef jerky, and fry, stirring, for a further 2 minutes.

4 Add the rice and cook for a few seconds, stirring everything together. Add enough boiling water to cover the ingredients by 2.5cm/1in and bring to the boil. Reduce the heat and cover the pan. Simmer the risotto for 15–20 minutes, or until the rice is tender and has absorbed all the liquid.

5 If the rice is not quite tender and there is no more liquid, add a few more tablespoons of just-boiled water and simmer for 2–3 minutes more until cooked.

6 Stir the chilli, parsley and spring onions into the rice. Taste and season with pepper. Serve straight away.

Serves 6–8

500g/1¼lb beef jerky
45ml/3 tbsp vegetable oil
115g/4oz bacon lardons
1 onion, finely chopped
3 cloves garlic, finely chopped
65g/2½oz smoked pork sausage such as kabanos, chouriço or chorizo
375g/13oz/generous 1½ cups easy-cook white rice
1 red chilli, seeded and very finely chopped
30ml/2 tbsp fresh parsley, chopped
2 spring onions (scallions), chopped
ground black pepper

A carreteiro was a wagon master who transported goods across the vast grasslands of the southern states of Brazil. His need for a hot meal that was easy to prepare and made from long-lasting ingredients created a recipe that would become synonymous with the profession and a symbol of the state of Rio Grande do Sul.

Grilled Rump Steak
Picanha fatiada

Serves 4

1 whole cut of beef rump cap, or picanha, about 1.25 kg/2½ lb in weight

30ml/2 tbsp coarse sea salt

white rice, Golden Farofa (page 48), and Brazilian-style Salsa (page 50), to serve

In Brazil's famous steakhouses, the churrascarias, picanha is one of the most sought-after cuts, cooked over the barbecue, then served in slices. True picanha aficionados prefer it served as a thick steak, seasoned with nothing but salt.

1 Rub the salt all over the beef, massaging it in. Leave at room temperature for 30 minutes.

2 Place the meat on a board, with the fat facing down and the narrower point of the triangular joint towards you. Check the direction in which the fibres run across the meat. The fibres should run diagonally from top-right to bottom-left or top-left to bottom-right. Placing your knife perpendicular to the fibres, cut the meat into 4–5cm/1½–2 in steaks; you should end up with four or five steaks.

3 Pat the steaks dry on both sides and grill (broil) them a very hot grill pan until done to your liking. Turn the steaks on their side for 1–2 minutes, to brown and sear the fat. Remove from the heat, place in a warm dish and cover. Allow to rest for 5–8 minutes.

4 Cut each steak into 1cm/½ in thick slices and serve with rice, farofa and salsa.

Pork Chops, Minas-style
Costeleta de porco à mineira

Serves 1

1 large pork chop or loin steak, about
    2.5cm/1in thick
juice of ½ lime
1 clove garlic, crushed
5ml/1 tsp olive oil
salt and ground black pepper
white rice and Brazilian-style
    Shredded Greens (page 46),
    to serve

1 Cut deep grooves into the fat on top of the meat, using a sharp knife. Whisk together the lime juice, garlic, olive oil and seasoning in a dish. Add the chop and rub in the marinade.

2 Set the chop aside at room temperature for up to 1 hour to allow the flavours to permeate the meat and mingle. Preheat the oven to 200°C/400°F/Gas 6.

3 Heat a griddle pan or heavy frying pan over a high heat and add the pork chop. Fry on each side for 1–2 minutes, until browned, then transfer to a shallow oven tray and bake for 10 minutes, until the fat and rind are crisp but the meat is still juicy.

4 Transfer to a warmed plate and serve with rice and shredded greens.

Whenever a dish is followed by the term 'à mineira', it means that it is from the state of Minas Gerais, and you can be sure it will be simple and hearty food. Here, pork chops are marinated to enhance the flavour and tenderize the meat before cooking.

Black Bean and Pork Stew
Feijoada

1 Put the pork ribs and the beef jerky in a large pan and cover with plenty of cold water. Bring to the boil and simmer for 45 minutes to 1 hour, replacing the water two or three times to remove the salt.

2 Drain the beef and pork. Cut the pork into separate ribs and cut the beef jerky into four or five large chunks.

3 Cut the smoked pork belly and smoked pork sausages into similar large chunks.

4 Place all the meat, together with the beans and bay leaves, in a clean pan and cover with fresh water. Bring to the boil, then lower the heat, cover, and simmer for 3–4 hours until the beans are almost cooked and the meats are soft. Top up with a little extra water, if needed, during the cooking time.

5 Heat the oil in a large frying pan and fry the onion and garlic for 10–12 minutes, stirring frequently, until they start to brown. Add to the bean and meat mixture.

6 Use some of the liquid from the beans to deglaze the frying pan and add back to the pan. Continue to simmer for a further 30 minutes, or until the meat and beans are very tender.

7 Garnish with sliced oranges and bacon lardons and serve piping hot, accompanied by polenta, shredded greens and with hot pepper sauce on the side.

Serves 12
300g/11oz salted smoked pork ribs
300g/11oz beef jerky
300g/11oz smoked pork belly
400g/14oz smoked pork sausages
    such as Portuguese paio or
    chouriço, or chorizo
1kg/2¼ lb dried black beans
3 bay leaves
45ml/3 tbsp vegetable oil
1 large onion, chopped
5 cloves garlic, chopped
6 oranges, peeled and sliced, and
    deep fried bacon lardons, to
    garnish
Brazilian-style Shredded Greens
    (page 46), Deep-fried Polenta
    (page 43) and hot pepper sauce,
    to serve

Feijoada is probably the best known Brazilian dish – possibly because it is the obvious menu choice when feeding a large crowd, and is often served at parties.

Sautéed Chayote Xuxu refogado

Serves 6

3 chayote
30ml/2 tbsp vegetable oil
1 small onion, finely chopped
15ml/1 tbsp butter
25g/1oz/½ cup parsley, finely
   chopped
salt and ground black pepper

1 Cut the chayote lengthways in half and rub the two halves together under cold running water (see Cook's tip). Cut away the white core and peel the prickly outer skin. Cut into 1cm/½in dice and set aside.

2 Heat the oil in a deep frying pan and fry the onion for 7–8 minutes, until soft and translucent. Add the chayote and butter and sauté for 3 or 4 minutes until shiny and tender when pierced with the tip of a knife.

3 Stir in most of the parsley and season to taste with salt and pepper. Sprinkle with the rest of the parsley and serve straight away.

COOK'S TIP
Some chayote have slightly sour sap in the middle, which needs to be drained away. Cutting in half, rubbing the halves together and rinsing under cold water is the easiest way to remove this. Young chayote don't need to be peeled; if the skin is pale and tender, you can leave it on.

The humble xuxu, or chayote, provides a light vegetable accompaniment for any meal. Its subtle taste works best when used in conjunction with well-flavoured ingredients, such as cooked beans, meat or chicken stews. Chayote grows throughout Brazil and is sold very cheaply in most supermarkets.

Deep-fried Polenta Polenta frita

Serves 6

1 litre/1¾ pints/4¼ cups water
325g/12½ oz/3¼ cups polenta
250ml/8fl oz/1 cup chicken stock
30ml/2 tbsp olive oil
30ml/2 tbsp plain (all-purpose) flour
vegetable oil, for deep-frying
salt

Polenta is made with ground yellow or white cornmeal. Here it is allowed to set, then deep-fried, giving it a deliciously crunchy texture. These chips can be served with all sorts of dishes, from roasted pork or chicken to stews and casseroles.

1 Pour the water into a large pan, with the polenta, stock and olive oil. Slowly bring to the boil, then simmer until it becomes a thick purée. The mixture is the correct consistency when the bottom of the pan starts to show as you stir. Sprinkle in the plain flour and continue cooking for another 3 minutes, stirring constantly.

2 Pour into an oiled 28 x 28cm/11 x 11 in tin (pan), using a spatula to spread into an even layer approximately 2.5cm/1 in thick. Cool, then chill in the refrigerator for 1 hour, until set.

3 Turn out the chilled block of polenta on to a lightly oiled board. Wet the blade of a knife and use it to cut into 6cm/2½ in long chips.

4 Half-fill a deep pan with oil, then heat to 190°C/375°F on a sugar thermometer. Add about a third of the chips to the oil, and fry for 3–4 minutes, until golden and crispy. Use a slotted spoon to remove them from the oil and drain on kitchen paper. Keep warm while cooking the remaining chips. Sprinkle with salt and serve straight away.

Everyday Black Beans Feijão simples

1 Put the beans and water in a pressure cooker, seal the lid and cook on a high heat until steam starts to escape. Lower the heat and cook for 40 minutes, until the beans are soft. (Always follow the manufacturer's instructions when using a pressure cooker.)

2 Heat the oil in a deep frying pan and fry the onion and garlic for 7–8 minutes, or until they start to brown.

3 Add a ladleful of beans and stock to the hot frying pan, and deglaze the pan by stirring together with the onion and garlic for a minute, scraping up any residue sticking to the base. Pour the mixture back into the rest of the beans in the pressure cooker.

4 Add the bay leaf to the beans, then simmer for a further 20 minutes, uncovered, until the onion is soft and the stock has reduced to a thick sauce. Remove the bay leaf and stir in the salt. If you prefer a thin sauce, add in a little boiling water.

5 Serve the beans straight away while still piping hot, as an accompaniment to a rice or meat dish.

COOK'S TIP
If you don't own a pressure cooker you will need to soak the beans overnight with enough water to cover them. The next day, drain the beans and transfer to a pan. Add 1 litre/1¾ pints/4 cups of water and simmer for 2–3 hours; top up with a little extra boiling water toward the end of cooking, if needed.

Brazilians eat a whole range of beans and pulses, but the black bean is by far the most popular. For many Brazilians this humble dish is everyday eating. High in protein and iron, this is an excellent economical dish which can be served to supplement a small portion of meat.

Serves 6
450g/1lb dried black beans
1.2 litres/2 pints/5 cups water
45ml/3 tbsp vegetable oil
1 onion, chopped
3 cloves garlic, finely chopped
1 bay leaf
5ml/1 tsp salt

Brazilian-style Shredded Greens
Couve à mineira

Serves 6

about 20 large leaves of spring
    greens (collards)
45ml/3 tbsp olive oil
4 cloves garlic, finely chopped
salt and ground black pepper

*Collard greens are a loose-
leaf plant very similar to kale
and spring greens, either of
which you can use as a
substitute, if necessary.
Grown throughout Brazil,
the leaves have a slightly
bitter taste and are excellent
with any rich meat dish.*

1 Carefully wash each leaf and cut off most of the thick part of the stalk.

2 Stack five or six leaves on top of each other and roll tightly. Cut into
very thin slices across the roll to make narrow strips of greens – the finer
the better.

3 Heat the olive oil in a large, deep frying pan or wok, add the garlic
and fry for a few seconds, then add the shredded greens. Stir for 5–6
minutes, until the greens have wilted and softened a little, but are still
slightly al dente. Add salt and pepper to taste and serve straight away.

COOK'S TIP

At first it may look as if you have a huge amount of greens, but these
lose a lot of volume and subside during cooking.

Deep-fried Straw Potatoes
Batata Palha

Serves 6

4 large potatoes, such as Maris Piper
or King Edward, peeled and cut
into very thin sticks
vegetable oil, for deep-frying
salt

1 Place the cut potato sticks in a large bowl of cold water to remove excess starch. Drain well, then transfer to a large, clean, dry dish towel and pat dry. Work in batches and change the dish towel when damp.

2 Half-fill a deep-fryer or pan with oil and heat to 190°C/375°F on a sugar thermometer. Fry in small batches for 2 or 3 minutes until soft. Transfer to an oven tray and leave to cool as you fry the other batches.

3 Wait until the oil has come back up to 190°C/375°F and fry the batches a second time. This time they should puff up in volume, and become golden in colour and very crunchy.

4 Using a slotted spoon, remove from the pan and transfer to a clean oven tray covered in kitchen paper.

COOK'S TIP

To save time, use a food mandolin or a julienne disc on your food processor to cut the potatoes.

5 Keep warm in a moderate oven while cooking the other batches. Sprinkle with salt and serve straight away.

These irresistible little fried potatoes are a popular Brazilian snack as well as a main meal accompaniment. They are available in supermarkets ready-made and foil-packed, but nothing can compare to the fresh hand-made version.

Golden Farofa Farofa amarela

Serves 6

30ml/2 tbsp vegetable oil
1 onion, finely chopped
115g/4oz/½ cup butter
30ml/2 tbsp palm oil (dendê)
500g/1¼lb/5 cups untoasted
   cassava flour
salt
1 egg, hard-boiled and sliced, and
   fresh coriander (cilantro), if you
   wish, to garnish

1 Heat the vegetable oil in a frying pan or a wok over a medium heat. Add the onion and fry for 7–8 minutes, until it is soft and translucent.

2 Add the butter to the pan and let it melt, then add the palm oil and mix together.

3 Add the cassava flour and stir slowly until the palm oil has coloured all the grains. Lower the heat and keep cooking for 3-4 minutes, until the farofa is golden and crunchy.

4 Season with salt, and serve, garnished with the slices of hard-boiled egg, and fresh coriander, if you wish.

This version of farofa is particularly well suited for fish dishes, especially if they are served with plenty of sauce. The farofa adds some crunch to the usual soft textures of fish, and then gradually absorbs the sauce. The rich nutty scent and deep yellow colour of the palm oil is a trademark of Afro-Brazilian cooking.

Brazilian-style Salsa Molho à campanha

Serves 6

1 green (bell) pepper, seeded
1 yellow (bell) pepper, seeded
3 plum tomatoes
1 large onion
100ml/3½fl oz/scant ½ cup white
   wine vinegar
200ml/7fl oz/scant 1 cup olive oil
25g/1oz/½ cup parsley, finely
   chopped
15ml/1 tbsp caster (superfine) sugar
2.5ml/½ tsp salt
2.5ml/½ tsp ground black pepper

1 Chop the peppers, tomatoes and onion into 1cm/½in dice and place in a large bowl.

2 Whisk together the vinegar, oil, parsley, sugar, salt and pepper in a small bowl. Pour over the chopped vegetables and stir well.

3 Serve immediately, or cover and chill in the refrigerator until you are ready to serve.

COOK'S TIP

The flavour of the salsa improves if it stands for 15 minutes or so, but it will lose its texture if you leave it for longer than 1 hour.

This simple fresh pepper, tomato and onion salsa is a wonderful accompaniment for any grilled meat. Barbecue aficionados claim that the combination of sharp acidic flavours is a good way to cleanse your palate between different cuts of meat.

Palm Heart Salad Salada de palmito

Serves 1–2

4 or 5 large palm heart stalks
2 ripe but firm plum tomatoes
1 large red onion
30ml/2 tbsp extra virgin olive oil
salt and ground black pepper
watercress or rocket (arugula) leaves,
    to garnish (optional)

Hearts of palm (palmito) are available fresh as well as conserved in jars or canned. Fresh ones are an expensive delicacy, but most Brazilians are happy to pay a little extra for meals containing palmito, which has found its way into hundreds of recipes.

1 Trim the ends of the palm heart stalks with a sharp knife to ensure they have flat ends, then cut each in half diagonally into two equal-sized wedge shapes.

2 Cut a slice from the base of the tomato and discard. Chop the tomato into quarters.

3 Slice the onion into rings. Select a few perfect rings. Save the rest for another recipe.

4 Arrange the palm hearts and tomatoes on a serving plate, top with the onion and add a few green leaves, if you wish. Finish with a drizzle of olive oil, and salt and pepper to taste.

Coconut and Egg Yolk Puddings Quindim

Makes 12

75g/3oz/generous ⅓ cup butter, melted, plus extra for greasing
225g/8oz/1 cup caster (superfine) sugar, plus extra for dusting
12 egg yolks
150g/5oz1½ cups fresh grated coconut

1 Preheat the oven to 150°C/300°F/Gas 2. Grease twelve small moulds, about 5cm/2 in wide, with a generous layer of butter, then sprinkle in enough sugar to cover all the butter in a light dusting. Tip out any excess.

2 Place the egg yolks in a fine sieve (strainer) and strain them into a large bowl. (Many Brazilian cooks strain their yolks, believing it makes them silkier.)

3 Add the sugar, grated coconut and melted butter to the egg yolks and mix well with a wooden spoon. Set aside for 20 minutes.

4 Stir the mixture again to combine, then divide between the moulds, filling them almost to the top with the coconut mixture.

5 Put the moulds in a roasting pan or oven dish, then pour in enough water to come halfway up the moulds. Bake for 45 minutes or until they are firm and the tops are lightly golden.

6 Remove the moulds from the hot water and leave them to cool for 10 minutes. Run a small blunt knife around the inside edges of each mould and turn the puddings out on to a large flat platter or small individual plates. Cool, then chill until ready to serve.

COOK'S TIP
Cooking the puddings in a dish of hot water (bain marie) ensures the puddings keep their delicate texture.

Any pudding or cake with this many eggs in the recipe is likely to be of Portuguese origin, but the addition of coconut gives the cakes a Caribbean flavour. Made with just four ingredients, these tiny glistening golden treats make a wonderful dessert or can be served with coffee.

Guava Soufflé
Soufflé de goiabada

1 Preheat the oven to 120°C/250°F/Gas ½. Put the goiabada and water in a small pan and gently heat until completely melted, stirring occasionally. Turn off the heat.

2 Whisk the egg whites together, in a large bowl, until stiff peaks form. Stir a spoonful of the egg whites into the melted guava mixture to loosen it a little, then pour the melted guava into the egg whites and gently fold in with a metal spoon.

3 Spoon the mixture into six 150ml/¼ pint/⅔ cup deep ramekins, then run a knife around the inside wall of the ramekins, which will help the soufflés to rise.

4 Place on an oven tray on the middle oven shelf, then turn up the oven temperature to 180°C/350°F/Gas 4 and bake for 15 minutes.

5 Meanwhile, gently heat the cream cheese and the milk together in a small pan, stirring occasionally until the cream cheese has melted. Pour into a small jug or bowl and leave to cool slightly.

6 Serve the soufflés straight away with the melted cream cheese.

Although guava is hugely popular in Brazil it is rarely eaten as a fresh fruit. Instead, it is boiled down with sugar to make a jellied guava paste, which is then dried into a solid, deep red block called goiabada. *The combination of a slice of* goiabada *and an equal-sized slice of fresh Minas cheese is Brazil's most popular dessert and is referred to as 'Romeo and Juliet'. This recipe for guava soufflé offers a less intense way of enjoying the fragrant flavour of* goiabada.

Serves 6

300g/11oz goiabada, cut into chunks
30ml/2 tbsp water
6 egg whites
300g/11oz/scant 1¼ cups cream cheese
250ml/8fl oz/1 cup milk

COOK'S TIP
If you find it difficult to find goiabada, this recipe also works well with Spanish membrillo or quince preserve.

Cassava Cake Bolo de aipim

1 Preheat the oven to 190°C/375°F/Gas 5. Grease and line the base of a 23cm/9in square cake tin (pan) with baking parchment.

2 In a large bowl, beat the butter and sugar together until the mixture looks crumbly. Add the yolks one by one, ensuring each is well incorporated before adding the next one.

3 Beat the egg mixture for 3–4 minutes, then add the grated coconut, cassava and milk and mix to combine.

4 Sift the flour into the bowl, and with a metal spoon, gently fold it into the egg mixture.

5 In a separate bowl, whisk the egg whites into stiff peaks, then add to the egg yolk and cassava mixture and carefully fold in.

6 Spoon the cake mixture into the prepared tin and bake for 40 minutes, or until golden-brown and firm. Remove from the oven and leave in the tin for 10 minutes before turning out and cooling on a wire rack.

Serves 12

20g/¾ oz/1½ tbsp butter, softened, plus extra for greasing
450g/1lb/2 cups caster (superfine) sugar
4 eggs, separated
100g/4oz/1 cup grated fresh coconut
300g/11oz cassava root, finely grated
250ml/8fl oz/1 cup milk
175g/6oz/1½ cups self-raising (self-rising) flour

This cake's rich flavour and fluffy texture is made even lighter with the addition of whisked egg whites, and it contains little fat. It is popular at carnivals held in June in the north of Brazil.

Egg Puffs in Sugar Syrup Papo de anjo

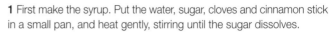

Serves 6

250ml/8fl oz/1 cup water

450g/1lb/2 cups caster (superfine) sugar

6 whole cloves

1 cinnamon stick

unsalted butter, softened, for greasing

1 whole egg

11 egg yolks

1 First make the syrup. Put the water, sugar, cloves and cinnamon stick in a small pan, and heat gently, stirring until the sugar dissolves.

2 Bring to the boil and simmer for 5 minutes to make a syrup. Turn off the heat and cover the pan with a lid. Leave to stand while making the egg puffs, so that the spices infuse the syrup. Preheat the oven to 160°C/325°F/Gas 3.

3 Lightly butter a 12–hole mini muffin tin (pan) or 12 small individual fixed-based tartlet tins (muffin pans), about 4cm/1½ in across.

4 Whisk the whole egg and egg yolks together in a bowl until pale and fluffy and doubled in size. Carefully divide the mixture between the muffin or tartlet tins.

5 Put the tins in a roasting pan and pour in enough very hot water to come almost halfway up the tins. Bake for 30 minutes until the tops of the puffs start to brown, then remove from the oven and stand on a wire rack to cool.

6 When the tins are cool enough to handle, run a small knife around the edges of each one to remove the egg puffs.

7 Place the puffs in a serving bowl, then pour the slightly warm syrup over the top. Leave for at least 15 minutes, to allow the little puffs to soak up the syrup, before serving.

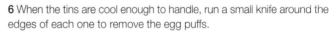

Like several other classical Portuguese desserts based on egg yolks, Papo de Anjo is believed to have been created by Portuguese monks and nuns during the 14th or 15th centuries. Laundry was a common service performed by convents and monasteries, and their use of egg whites for starching clothes created a surplus of yolks.

Rolled Sponge Cake with Guava Filling
Rocambole de goiabada

1 Line the base and short sides of a shallow 38 x 30cm/15 x 12 in cake tin (pan) with a single strip of baking parchment. The two long sides of the tin should be buttered and then dusted with flour.

2 If using goiabada for the filling, cut into small chunks, and place in a pan with 60ml/4 tbsp water. Gently heat the goiabada, stirring, until melted. Set aside. Preheat the oven to 180°C/350°F/Gas 4.

3 In a large bowl, whisk the egg yolks and sugar together until they are pale and thick.

4 In a separate bowl whisk the egg whites until stiff peaks form. Fold into the yolk mixture, then sift the flour over the mixture and fold in.

5 Transfer the cake mixture to the prepared tin and bake for 25 minutes, or until it turns a very light brown and springs back when lightly pressed. Remove from the oven and let it cool in the tin for 10 minutes.

6 Lay a clean dish towel on the worktop and sprinkle with caster sugar. Turn out the sponge on to the towel. Trim 1cm/½ in of cake off the two long edges.

7 Spread the melted goiabada, or other filling, over the sponge in a thin layer. Hold one end of the towel with both hands and use it to roll the cake from one of the short sides to the other.

8 Transfer to a serving plate, seam-side down, dust with sugar and serve. It is delicious with whipped cream or crème fraiche.

COOK'S TIP
It is important to trim off the long sides or the sponge will be difficult to roll and may crack.

Serves 8
For the sponge:
8 eggs, separated
80g/3oz/scant ⅔ cup caster (superfine) sugar
75g/2¾oz/generous ½ cup self raising (self-rising) flour

For the filling:
250g/9oz jam, goiabada or dulce de leche
45ml/3 tbsp caster (superfine) sugar, for sprinkling

A truly international creation, this recipe has a French name, a Portuguese sponge and a Brazilian filling. Rocambole is a rolled cake made with pão de ló, an egg-rich cake mixture made with no butter, which gives it a very light and springy texture.

Hominy Corn Porridge Mugunzá

Serves 8

250g/9oz/1½ cups hominy corn
115g/4oz/½ cup caster (superfine)
    sugar
400ml/14fl oz/1⅔ cups coconut milk
5ml/1 tsp salt, or to taste
4 whole cloves
2 sticks cinnamon
250ml/8fl oz/1 cup milk (optional)

To serve:

15ml/1 tbsp ground cinnamon
115g/4 oz/⅔ cups raw peanuts,
    chopped
8 sticks cinnamon (optional)

*Mugunzá is made from
hominy, a bleached corn
(maize) product, originally
from Central America.
Adopted by the Candomblé
religion, still practised by
African descendants in Brazil,
hominy is used as an offering
to their gods. Mugunzá is
enjoyed during winter, and in
the south, where it is known
as 'cangica'.*

1 Put the hominy in a bowl, cover with cold water, and leave to soak for at least 8 hours, or overnight, if preferred. Drain well, then tip into a large pan and pour over enough water to cover. Bring to the boil, reduce the heat, cover, and simmer for 1 hour, until tender. Drain again.

2 Return to the pan and add the sugar, coconut milk, salt, cloves and cinnamon sticks. Simmer for 40–60 minutes, stirring occasionally, especially near the end of the cooking time.

3 Add extra milk, if needed, during cooking, to keep the mixture from becoming too thick.

4 Serve the porridge hot, in bowls, garnished with a sprinkling of cinnamon, chopped peanuts, and a stick of cinnamon, if liked.

Nutritional notes

Green Broth: Energy 328kcal/1366kJ; Protein 10.7g; Carbohydrate 25.5g, of which sugars 5.4g; Fat 21g, of which saturates 5g; Cholesterol 0mg; Calcium 138mg; Fibre 6 g; Sodium 276mg

Black Bean Pick-me-up: Energy 320kcal/1333kJ; Protein 21.3g; Carbohydrate 8.6g, of which sugars 1.8g; Fat 22.5g, of which saturates 0.7g; Cholesterol 0mg; Calcium 48mg; Fibre 14.1g; Sodium 746mg

Deep-fried Chunky Cassava Chips: Energy 295kcal/1237kJ; Protein 0.7g; Carbohydrate 41.4g, of which sugars 1.7g; Fat 15.2g, of which saturates 1.2g; Cholesterol 0mg; Calcium 21mg; Fibre 1.9g; Sodium 1971mg

Salt Cod Fritters: Energy 100kcal/414kJ; Protein 6.5g; Carbohydrate 3.5, of which sugars 0.1g; Fat 6.5g, of which saturates 0.9g; Cholesterol 28mg; Calcium 47mg; Fibre 0.3g; Sodium 804mg

Deep-fried Pastry with Cheese Filling: Energy 278kcal/1167kJ; Protein 10.3g; Carbohydrate 33.7g, of which sugars 0.7g; Fat 12.3g, of which saturates 6.7g; Cholesterol 24mg; Calcium 181mg; Fibre 1.6g; Sodium 461mg

Stuffed Baked Crabs: Energy 208kcal/869kJ; Protein 12.6g; Carbohydrate 12g, of which sugars 1.7g; Fat 12.5g, of which saturates 5.5g; Cholesterol 52mg; Calcium 89mg; Fibre 1.1g; Sodium 420mg

Seafood and Nut Purée: Energy 302/1268kJ; Protein 15.3g; Carbohydrate 32.5g, of which sugars 6.7g; Fat 13.2g, of which saturates 3.4g; Cholesterol 45mg; Calcium 245mg; Fibre 2.7g; Sodium 878mg

Leão Veloso Fish Soup: Energy 367kcal/1545kJ; Protein 62.6g; Carbohydrate 5.5g, of which sugars 2.2g; Fat 10.7g, of which saturates 1.8g; Cholesterol 239mg; Calcium 178mg; Fibre 0.9g; Sodium 883mg

Salt Cod and Potatoes: Energy 551kcal/2292kJ; Protein 35.1g; Carbohydrate 26.2g, of which sugars 11.2g; Fat 34.1g, of which saturates 6.5g; Cholesterol 87mg; Calcium 437mg; Fibre 3.4g; Sodium 4372mg

Chicken and Prawn Stew: Energy 419kcal/1751kJ; Protein 41.9g; Carbohydrate 10.4g, of which sugars

8.5g; Fat 23.7g, of which saturates 5.9g; Cholesterol 253mg; Calcium 190mg; Fibre 2g; Sodium 808mg

Beef Jerky Risotto: Energy 485kcal/2055kJ; Protein 5.5g; Carbohydrate 101g, of which sugars 1.4g; Fat 9.3g, of which saturates 1.9g; Cholesterol 0mg; Calcium 63mg; Fibre 1.6g; Sodium 52mg

Grilled Rump Steak: Energy 781kcal/3288kJ; Protein 137.5g; Carbohydrate 0g, of which sugars 0g; Fat 25.6g, of which saturates 10.6g; Cholesterol 369mg; Calcium 26mg; Fibre 0g; Sodium 4305mg

Pork Chops, Minas-style: Energy 436kcal/1820kJ; Protein 44g; Carbohydrate 0.8g, of which sugars 0.3g; Fat 28.7g, of which saturates 9.1g; Cholesterol 129mg; Calcium 35mg; Fibre 0.5g; Sodium 304mg

Black Bean and Pork Stew: Energy 547kcal/2305kJ; Protein 33g; Carbohydrate 63.5g, of which sugars 4.2g; Fat 20g, of which saturates 6g; Cholesterol 30mg; Calcium 95mg; Fibre 19.8g; Sodium 688mg

Sautéed Chayote: Energy 85kcal/353kJ; Protein 0.9g; Carbohydrate 4.6g, of which sugars 3.7g; Fat 7.2g, of which saturates 1.9g; Cholesterol 5mg; Calcium 23mg; Fibre 2.3g; Sodium 173mg

Deep-fried Polenta: Energy 300kcal/1248kJ; Protein 5.6g; Carbohydrate 42.7g, of which sugars 0.1g; Fat 12.2g, of which saturates 1.3g; Cholesterol 0mg; Calcium 17mg; Fibre 0.2g; Sodium 161mg

Everyday Black Beans: Energy 233kcal/982kJ; Protein 13.3g; Carbohydrate 27.9g, of which sugars 2.9g; Fat 8.4g, of which saturates 1.0g; Cholesterol 0mg; Calcium 65mg; Fibre 0.5g; Sodium 179mg

Brazilian-style Shredded Greens: Energy 97kcal/399kJ; Protein 2.7g; Carbohydrate 2.9g, of which sugars 2.3g; Fat 8.3g, of which saturates 1.2g; Cholesterol 0mg; Calcium 175mg; Fibre 5.1g; Sodium 82mg

Deep-fried Straw Potatoes: Energy 280kcal/1163kJ; Protein 2.8g; Carbohydrate 22.9g, of which sugars 0.8g; Fat 20.2g, of which saturates 2.3g; Cholesterol 0mg; Calcium 7mg; Fibre 2.1g; Sodium 173mg

Golden Farofa: Energy 549kcal/2301kJ; Protein 2g; Carbohydrate 78.8g, of which sugars 1.5g; Fat 27.3g, of which saturates 13.3g; Cholesterol 73mg; Calcium 27mg; Fibre 0.4g; Sodium 237mg

Brazilian-style Salsa: Energy 346kcal/1430kJ; Protein 1.5g; Carbohydrate 9.4g, of which sugars 8.3g; Fat 33.7g, of which saturates 4.8g; Cholesterol 0mg; Calcium 23mg; Fibre 2.3g; Sodium 173mg

Palm Heart Salad: Energy 204kcal/843kJ; Protein 2.8g; Carbohydrate 13.6g, of which sugars 10.5g; Fat 15.7g, of which saturates 2.3g; Cholesterol 0mg; Calcium 48mg; Fibre 4.3g; Sodium 209mg

Coconut and Egg Yolk Puddings: Energy 254kcal/1060kJ; Protein 8.2g; Carbohydrate 138.3g, of which sugars 110.7g; Fat 9.1g, of which saturates 5.5g; Cholesterol 30mg; Calcium 384mg; Fibre 4.8g; Sodium 275mg

Guava Soufflé: Energy 341kcal/1414kJ; Protein 11.1g; Carbohydrate 4.5g, of which sugars 4.4g; Fat 31.2g, of which saturates 17.2g; Cholesterol 282mg; Calcium 141mg; Fibre 2.4g; Sodium 256mg

Cassava Cake: Energy 357kcal/1523kJ; Protein 4.5g; Carbohydrate 73.9g, of which sugars 40.1g; Fat 6.8g, of which saturates 4.1g; Cholesterol 81mg; Calcium 77mg; Fibre 2.3g; Sodium 94mg

Egg Puffs in Sugar Syrup: Energy 436kcal/1841kJ; Protein 6.7g; Carbohydrate 78.8g, of which sugars 78.8g; Fat 12.6g, of which saturates 4.1g; Cholesterol 416mg; Calcium 57mg; Fibre 0g; Sodium 45mg

Rolled Sponge Cake with Guava Filling: Energy 118kcal/794kJ; Protein 8.8g; Carbohydrate 24.6g, of which sugars 18.1g; Fat 6.8g, of which saturates 1.9g; Cholesterol 232mg; Calcium 72mg; Fibre 1.8g; Sodium 119mg

Hominy Corn Porridge: Energy 192kcal/812kJ; Protein 4.1g; Carbohydrate 41.4g, of which sugars 19g; Fat 1.9g, of which saturates 0.4g; Cholesterol 2mg; Calcium 59mg; Fibre 0g; Sodium 315mg

Index